Joe Petrosino's

War on the Mafia

Illustrated

Lieutenant Joe Petrosino, NYCPD. Born 1861 - Died 1909, age 48

Giuseppe Petrosino, who went by the Americanized name Joe Petroseena, was born in Padula near Salerno, Italy on August 30th 1860. His family emigrated to America in 1873. Young Petrosino decided to become a cop after shining patrolmen's shoes outside of police headquarters on Mulberry Street.

Mulberry Street

In his teens applied to the Irish dominated force but was rejected. "He was too short, too swarthy, spoke with an accent and wasn't Irish".

An Italian woman 'rag-picker' in her living space, with her packs of junk, few possessions including her straw hat hung on the wall behind her, and a child in her lap.

In 1878 Petrosino became a City street sweeper and won a promotion to foreman within a year. In 1879, Petrosino got a break when Police Captain Alexander "Clubber" Williams was assigned to command the street cleaning department.

Tenement life in New York for some Italian immigrants

The New York City Police force if the mid nineteenth-century was full of goons, enforcers, thieves and extortionists.

Aftermath of a Blackhand terrorist bombing

Some precincts were richer than others and offered more "graft and gravy" and for the many crooked cops on the force, the idea was to get assigned to the more lucrative areas such as the 29th, the fashionable red-light district on the West Side below 42nd Street.

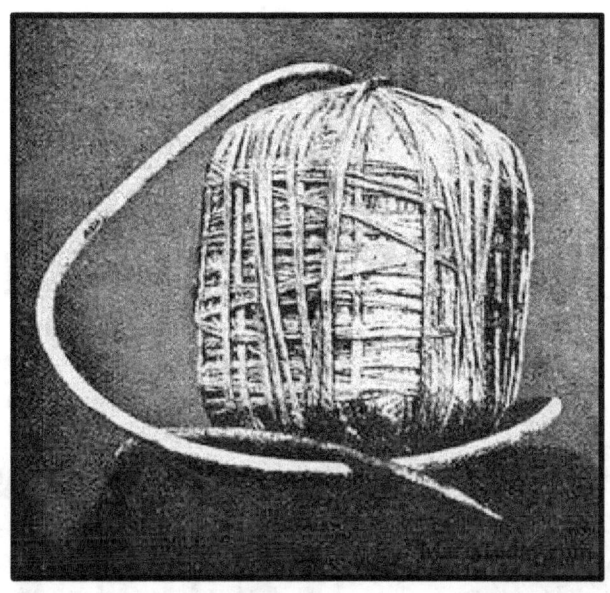

Blackhand dynamite bomb

Here, the sex trade was protected by the police who in turn paid off the local political machine, Tammany. In 1876, when police Capt. Alexander "Clubber" Williams was transferred there with the announcement "Boy's I've had nothing but chuck steak for a long time, and now I'm going to get a little of the tenderloin." And hence the Tenderloin was named.

Street scene after a Blackhand bomb destroyed a New York Bank

One of Brooklyn's Italian immigrant ghetto's

Williams was brutal, thoroughly corrupt cop. "There is" he once said "more law at the end of a policeman's nightstick than in all the decisions of the Supreme Court" Police wouldn't be armed until 1877 and Williams had a reputation as a man who knew how to handle himself and his police club (Then called a paddy club) When William's joined the force in the late 1860s, he decided to clean up the areas along Broadway and Houston Streets. He started by beating two local gang members unconscious and throwing them through the plate-glass window of the Florence Saloon.

Clubber Williams (left) and a Blackhand threat nailed to a shop keepers door

Blackhanders deported to Italy

Six other members of the gang rushed out of the saloon only to meet William, standing alone, club in hand. He beat them all to a pulp with his club. Remarkably, as corrupt as he was, Williams was promoted to the rank of Captain in 1871 and later an inspector.

Black handers and police interpreter (center)

Yet witnesses before an 1894 investigation into police graft claimed the Clubber was receiving $30,000 a year, at a time when a police captain earned less than $200 a month, in protection money from one brothel alone.

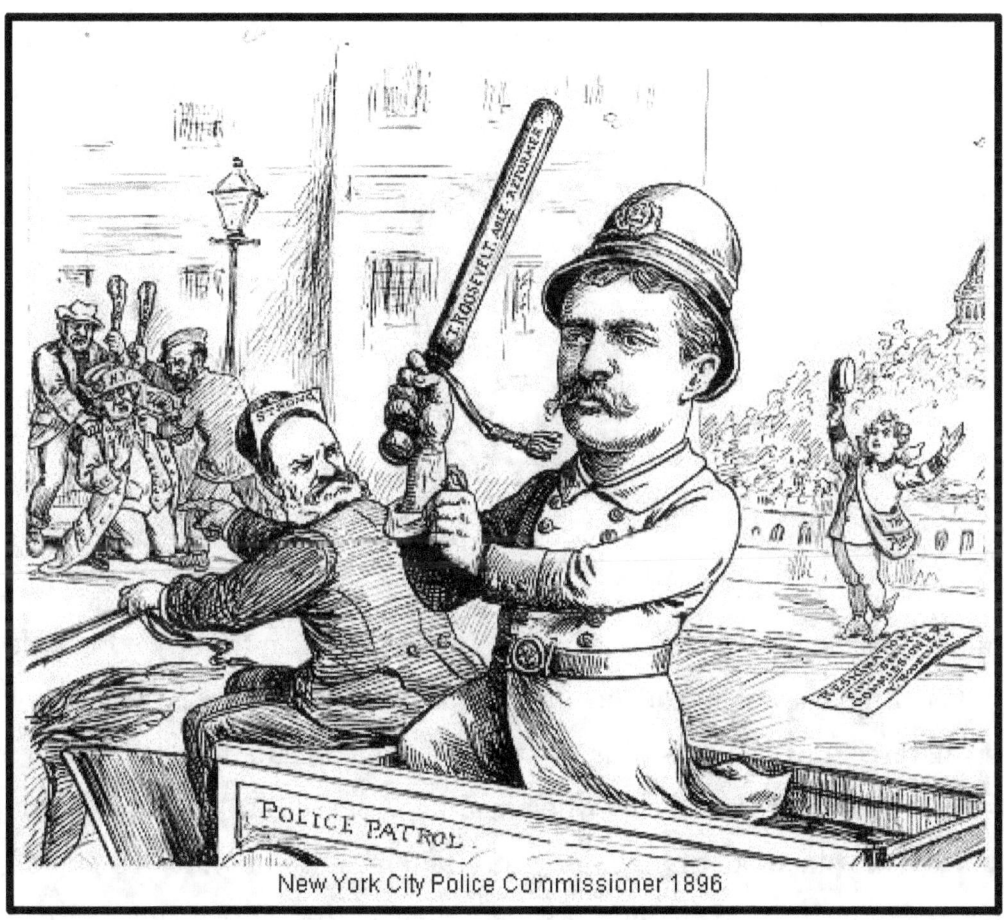
New York City Police Commissioner 1896

The investigation also discovered that he owned an enormous estate and 17 room mansion in fashionable Cos Cobb Connecticut, a 53-foot yacht, a considerable fortune in cash and commercial real estate. When asked to explain his wealth, the Clubber explained that he had made his fortune through real estate speculation in Japan. Police Commissioner Teddy Roosevelt forced Williams into retirement shortly afterwards.

Williams liked Petrosino's intelligence, toughness and industry and in 1883, arranged Joe's appointment to the force, even though Petrosino was four inches below the required height. Due to his fluency in every Italian dialect, and knowledgeable of underworld, he rose through the ranks quickly and was soon known as the City's leading Italian American officer in a department dominated by the Irish. Neighborhood toughs constantly challenged him when he first started foot patrol until word got around he was not a man to be taken lightly.

Petrosino

One night a Black man named Washington was jumped on the street by three thugs. Petrosino was on patrol and entered the fight. When it was over, they had beaten all three thugs unconscious. He was a tough cop and not above using his fists to get the answers he needed when dealing with the Black Hand, extortionist who sucked the blood out of the immigrant Italian community. It was said of Petrosino that he had "taken out more teeth then all the dentists in New York"

He was comfortable in disguise, posing as a tunnel worker, a blind beggar, a gangster or an Italian peasant just off the boat. The outfits allowing him to investigate freely, and also allowed others to talk to him without attracting suspicion. In this way he was able to infiltrate and expose many of the gangs that preyed on Italian immigrants.

He had a heart. When he was required him to arrest low level hoods, many of whom left their innocent families destitute, Petrosino would check up on them. One of them became one of his most important informers later on out of gratitude. Through careful media management, Petrosino was one of New York's best-known detectives: he had a way of tipping off reporters whenever he was about to do something newsworthy. And he was newsworthy. Petrosino had flash and style to go along with his guts.

1º Marzo

Preparati per la tua morte

Primera e Ultima

Blackhand warning to a shopkeeper

One Blackhand victim recalled. "When I was a child, I had been kidnapped by the Black Hand. I was kept in a room by a man and a woman. The woman used to come in to feed me and wash me. One night, as I was in bed, I saw the skylight being lifted and a rope came down. All of a sudden a man climbed down the rope. As I looked up in terror, he motioned to me with his finger over his lips not to scream. When he reached the floor, he showed me his badge, whispered to me he was detective Petrosino, caressed me, told me not to be afraid and made me hide under the bed. When my kidnappers turned on the light and entered the room, he arrested them."

Enrico "Erricone (Big Henry)" Alfano was a Mafioso who found his way to New York and bragged that he would personally kill Petrosino. On April 17, 1907, Petrosino found Alfano at lunch with his gang and several Mafia leaders. Petrosino lifted him up by the nape of the neck and threw him into two thugs who had made the mistake of drawing their pistols on the cop. They were beaten senseless and Alfano was dragged through the streets of Little Italy on his knees all the way to police headquarters. He was deported several days later. He also arrested Enrico Costabili, the head of the New York Camorra and also shot and had deported Giovanni Campanillo, another Camorrist.

Blackhanders

Early photo of Lupo the Wolf and a later shot

Lupo the Wolf, the most feared Mafia killer in the city, had also sworn to kill the cop, referring to him as "This troublesome sbirro (flatfoot) Unfortunately for Lupo, Petrosino got word of the threat. Petrosino tracked the wolf down to a store in Little Italy in mid-day. There were heated words and Lupo spat at the cop calling him a Son of bitch.

Petrosino punched Lupo to the floor and then kicked him out on to the street where a crowd watched the beating which ended with the cop tossing the hood into a trash can and turning to the crowd and asking "Is this the coward you are all so afraid of? How tough does he look now?" The press dubbed Petrosino the "Detective in the Derby Hat" a particular style that hide his baldness and to compensate for his lack of height somewhere in or about 5 foot 2 to five foot 6.

LIVES OF 10,000 IN PERIL BY BLACK HAND, BINGHAM HELPLESS

Citizens Menaced by Bands Organized for Murder, Kidnapping and Extortion Without Hindrance From 8,000 Police of City.

In 1890, Petrosino was assigned to investigate the Italian underworld and promoted to a sergeant of detectives by the president of the Police Commission board, Theodore Roosevelt.

The police department, in some part due to simply lazy police work initially labeled all Italian organized crime as the Black Hand, which was actually a method of operation rather than an organization. Petrosino knew better, it was the Mafia that they were dealing with. As Petrosino documented, the Mafia had been active in New York since at least 1857, when police officer Eugene Anderson was beaten to death by Mike Cancemi, a known mob operative.

Petrosino promotion to lead the Italian squad (Above with Petrosino standing left) was perfect. During the 1890s, the Italian government placed Sicily under martial law for two years and stepped on the local Mafia Don's, many of whom simply emigrated to the United States.

By 1891, the all-powerful Ignazio Saietta, AKA Lupo the Wolf, (Above) and his partner/Underboss Giuseppe Morello, were running a tightly knit Mafia family in New York, specializing in counterfeiting, extortion and running a "murder factory", their term for the operation, on E. 107th St. At least sixty murders have been attributed to the Lupo gang. The office, or murder factory, was also the headquarters for the Unione Siciliana.

Morello in a later mug shot

In 1901, Petrosino searched the headquarters of the Unione Siciliana and discovered the bodies and body parts of approximately 60 murder victims hidden around the building. Lupo the Wolf was arrested, on the grounds that he owned the building, but there was no evidence to link him to the crimes. Giuseppe Morello may have been born in 1870, the exact date is unknown, to an established Mafia family in Corleone, Sicily.

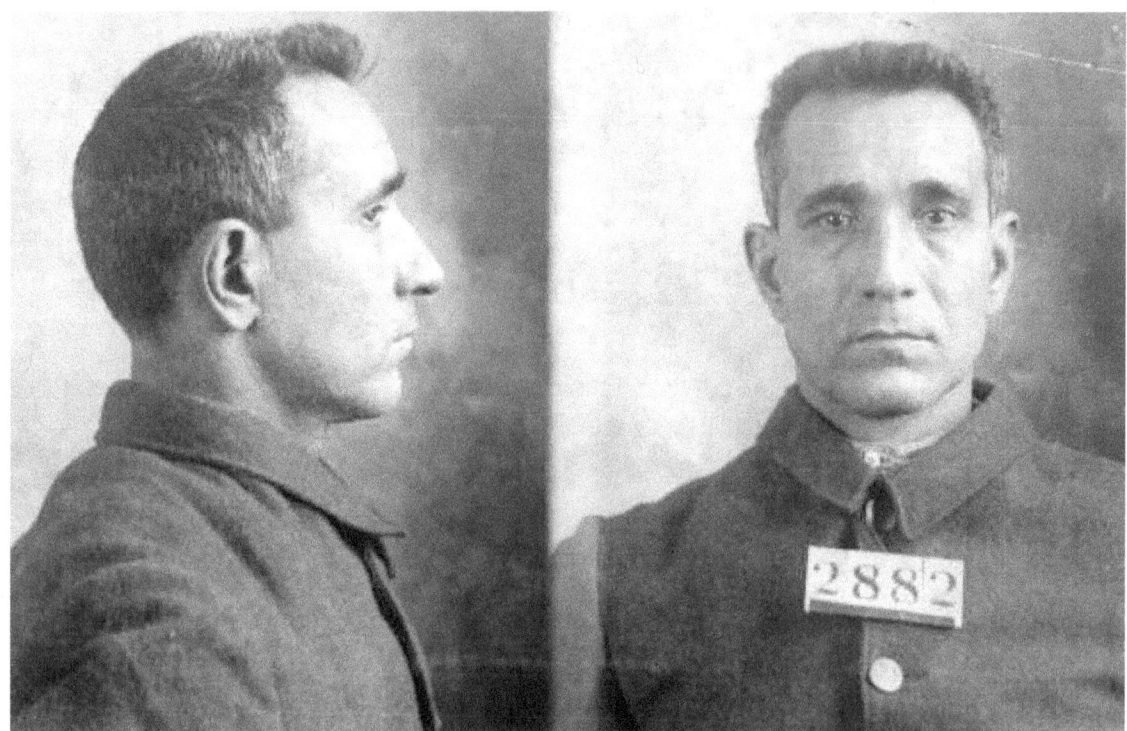

Morello's prison mug shot

The family moved to New York City on or around 1892, settling in East Harlem. The Morello father and oldest brother, Antonio, were killed in shootouts before 1900. With his brother Antonio the Morello's quickly organized what became the 107th Street Mob in East Harlem.

Morello

In a short time, the gangs power extended into Brooklyn. When Antonio was killed, Giuseppe Morello took over and quickly came to the attention of Ignazio Lupo, Mafia boss over Manhattan's Lower East Side and also a power in Brooklyn. By 1900, Morello and Lupo were in business together.

Another Capo in the gang was Giuseppe Fontana, the alleged assassin of the Marquis Emanuele di Notarbartolo who had uncovered the massive banking scandal in the Bank of Sicily at the end of the 19th century. In 1893, he was on a train heading for court where he was to testify against Raffaele Palizzuolo the "King of the Mafia" in Palermo and deputy member of Sicily's Parliament. On Palizzuolo's orders, Fontana, together with Carlo Costantino stabbed the nobleman to death and threw his body onto the tracks.

Benditto Madonia

In April of 1903, police discovered the body of Benditto Madonia stuffed into a barrel at Ave. A and 11th St. The corpse had 18 stab wounds; the throat had been slit; the penis and testicles had been shoved into his mouth, suggesting that he had been a police informer. The throat was cut from ear to ear, the head almost severed from eighteen stab wounds in the neck. The body had been forcibly pushed into the barrel with the head resting between the knees. The coroner concluded that stab wounds to the neck were inflicted before the killing cut to the jugular vein, this meant he was either attacked in his sleep or restrained as he was tortured. In his pocket was a piece of paper, upon which was written 'Come at Once!' in Italian. Madonia's body could have been tossed into the East River, quietly, but it wasn't, the killers wanted it to be discovered, they wanted to send a message.

Petrosino was assigned to the case and traced the barrel to a firm of confectioners who had shipped it to an Italian cafe on Elizabeth Street, a rendezvous for counterfeiters.

Elizabeth Street

Petrosino also learned that Madonia had known Giuseppe De Priemo, a counterfeiter who was already in Sing Sing prison. (Below)

De Priemo was Madonia's brother-in-law. In 1902, De Primo who was found in possession of counterfeit $5 bills. The plates from which the bills were printed had been stolen earlier in the year from the National Bank of Morristown, New Jersey. The story that Petrosino was able to put together was that De Priemo had sent Madonia to collect money owed him by Joe Morello, who refused to pay. So Madonia threatened to go to the police. Although a more likely story is that Madonia had tried to establish a competitive counterfeiting ring to the Lupo-Morella organization and paid with his life for his mistake.

In 1908, Giuseppe De Primo, the convict who implicated Lupo and Morella in the murder of his brother-in-law Madonia, was released from prison and deported to Sicily. Vito Laduca, a onetime New York Black Hander deported back to Sicily three years before DePrimo's arrival there, was contracted to take care of business. However

Laduca wasn't much of a contract killer. Police found his body, shot to death, on a roadside. Cops suspected the killers were the Morello gang. The US Secret Service had been tracking the Morello gang for over a year on suspicion of counterfeiting in a ring that extended to New Orleans, Buffalo, Pittsburgh and Chicago.

Eight members of the gang were arrested in the Bowery and working on a tip probably provided by one of the eight men, police located the murder scene, a pastry shop, the Café Pasticceria run by Pietro Inzerillo,a Morello gang member. On Thursday April 16th, four more Morello men were arrested in connection with the murder including Ignazio Lupo, AKA Lupo the wolf. Cops found a dagger and three revolvers hidden in the apartment. In the meantime, attempts were still being made to identify the murder victim. Lupo was questioned in his cell about the murder in Sicily that he was wanted for, and he openly admitted to the killing. In the meantime, the Secret Service was securing its case to arrest Lupo for counterfeiting should he escape the barrel killing arrest. They also planned to pin another murder on Lupo based on evidence found during the raid on his apartment on the day he was arrested.

JOSEPH CATANIA

Lupo was the last man seen with Joseph Catania, a Brooklyn grocer who was killed. His body, sewn in to a sack, was found at Bay Ridge in July 1902. Catania was believed to have been involved in counterfeiting with the gang before his murder.

Petrosino(left) , Inspector Carey and Inspector McCafferty Petto the Ox (Tomasso Petto, second from left)

Word reach the cop that a hood from the Lupo-Morello gang, Tomas "the Ox" Petto, was spreading around a lot of money. Petrosino and several of his squad members tracked the Ox down and told him they were taking him in questioning. Stupidly the Ox pulled a knife. Fighting Petto, even without a knife was no small venture.

He had won prizes in Italy for his remarkable physique and was dubbed "The Ox" ("il Bue") and sometimes "The Bull" by his fellow criminals. The Detectives beat him viciously and found a second knife, a pistol and a pawn ticket in his pockets for Madonia's watch. Now they had evidence. The New York Police arrested 9 men in connection with the murder: Joe Morello, Ignazio Saietta, Giuseppe Fontano, Tony Genoa, Giuseppe Favarro, Giovanni Pecoraro, Vito Lo Baido, Vito Cascio Ferro and Gaetano Petto. Vito Cascio Ferro was no minor crook. He was, during his life, a legendary Mafia chieftain and the first Sicilian to be considered capo di tutti capi, Boss of Bosses.

Ferro had arrived in the US in 1900 he moved in with his sister over a shop on 103rd Street and went about the business of building a massive extortion business in the Italian community. Payments were made weekly, allowing Ferro not only a steady income but the ability to build up a family, a regime, inside the United States. He was born in 1862 at Bisacquino, near Palermo, the son of illiterate peasants.

His criminal record included assault, extortion, arson and a fumbled plot to kidnap the Baroness di Valpetrosa in 1899. Released on bail Ferro skipped and eventually the witnesses changed their stories and the case died. As for The Ox Petto, who had obviously ratted out on Lupo and the others, he was found dead within two years, a knife rammed through his heart. Petrosino tracked Ferro to New Orleans, where he slipped away ultimately returning to Italy in 1904, his dream of becoming Capo di tutti i capi in America forever thwarted by an honest cop. When Ferro left, he took a picture of Petrosino and kept it in his wallet and swore that he would kill Petrosino with his own hands. Back in Sicily Ferro dominated crime there. Nothing, absolutely nothing, went down without his consent and percentage. Even beggars had to contribute a regular percentage of their daily collections.

Petrosino

The Lupo-Morella gang stayed active for five more years. In 1905, an extortionist named Michael Savona tried to extort payoffs from a barber named Andrea Gambino who turned out to be related to Joe Morella. When Savona returned for his money, Gambino shot him in the head killing him. That same year, a Brooklyn butcher Gaetano Costa refused to pay protection money to Lupo the wolf. Costa was beaten and murdered. In the meantime, Petrosino founded the Bomb Squad, the first unit of its kind in the United States, to counter the Black Hand's use of explosives in carrying out its extortion threats. From 1905, Petrosino and the "Italian Branch," (Later changed to the Italian Legion) an elite corps of Italian-American undercover cops, arrested thousands of members of the Black Hand, deported 500 and reduced crime against Italian-Americans by half.

In 1905, answering demands by Itlo-American business men, the New York Board of Aldermen agreed to the formation of a squad of exclusively Italian-American policemen. Petrosino was placed on the squad of course, and immediately set up an intelligence network within Little Italy, Using a massive network of citizens, businessmen, hoods, prostitutes and spies he built a hug system of intelligence files on the Mafia active in New York. Two years later, with success already in place, in 1906, New York's Police Commissioner, Teddy Bingham, threw the weight of the New York City Police Department behind the Italian squad.

Bingham

Bingham leads the St. Patrick's Day Parade

Within four months the unit grew from five members to twenty five, plus a second detachment of ten men in Brooklyn under the command of Antonio Vachris and Petrosino was promoted to Lieutenant.

Antonio Vachris

Still, Petrosino was frustrated by the Mafia's ability to avoid deportation. Cases were dismissed on technicalities as quickly as Petrosino could arrest the criminals. One problem was that the police department, including the Italian Unit, was drenched with spies working for the mob. Commissioner Bingham and Petrosino decided that the only way the unit could be successful was if it operated in secret and slightly outside the law. In December of 1908, Bingham created a secret branch of the Italian unit, headed by Petrosino. The unit wouldn't take any city money, instead it would be funded by the Italian American business community.

DEATH
TO
PETRO SINO

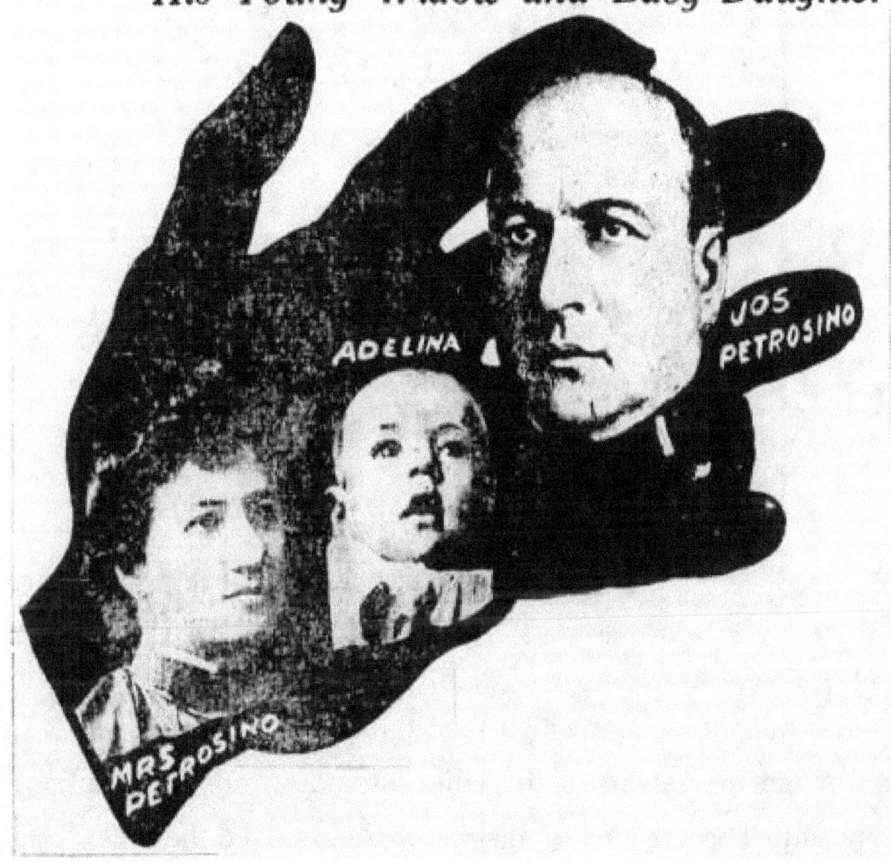

Detective Killed by Black Hand in Italy,
His Young Widow and Baby Daughter

In 1907, Congress enacted a law permitting the deportation of any alien found to have concealed a criminal record, meaning that if the Italian Squad could deliver proof that New York's Mafia members held criminal records in Europe, they could be deported without question. The other reason for the trip may have been to set up an espionage ring in Sicily so that the Police would have information on the comings and goings in Palermo as well as those between Palermo and the U.S., specifically New Orleans and New York. Commissioner Bingham, liked the idea and assigned Petrosino the difficult task of laying the groundwork for the spy network until a replacement arrived.

 It was a bad choice and Petrosino knew it. He was too well-known and had incurred the enmity of too many high-placed Mafioso. He didn't want to go. Petrosino who married late in life to a childless widow, Adelina (Saulino) Vinti in 1907, had recently become a father just before he received the order to sail to Italy. His daughter was two months old when he was murdered and never knew her father. He had no desire to leave this family. Petsoino traveled to Italy in February 1908 to collect criminal record and proof of imprisonment on mobsters. He carried a list of 2000 names in a note book that he intended to check out.

Antonio Passananti

Sailing to Sicily around the same time as Petrosino, were Carlo Costantino and Antonio Passananti. Costantino had been the stand in look-alike for Petto, causing the 'Barrel Murder' case to fall apart.

Carlo Costantino

The mission was supposed to be secret, but before Petrosino set foot in Italy his travel's were front page news, in the United States and Italy. Bingham leaked news of the mission to the New York Herald, which published it in the Paris edition. The Italian press picked it up. Petrosino's impending visit and its purpose were known to the very Mafiosi he was investigating before his arrival. In his statement, Bingham told a reporter that Petrosino was on a "Secret mission" For years, Bingham, who lived under the cloud that he had sold Petrosino out to the mob, claimed that he had made the statement to a report but off the record and that the reporter betrayed his confidence. The fact was that if the mafia wanted to know about Petrosino's arrival and to have him followed, they didn't need Bingham's assistance. They knew of Petrosino's arrival and subsequent journey every step of the way.

The mission was simply too big a job for one man pitted alone against the entire might of the Mafia and he knew it. Petrosino wrote to his wife Adelina that he was being "followed everywhere" and later sent her a telegram from Noto, Sicily stating "It is very uncomfortable to be here alone."

He had never hidden from the mob. "The quickest way to be assassinated" he told his parish priest "is to hide." Yet he knew he would be killed. Newly arrived Mafia thugs were taken to Police headquarters where Petrosino would be pointed out to them. One day he told another cop "I know they'll get me. It's just a matter of time. But someone has to stand up to these bastards or they'll grind our people into the Earth."

Alfano and other Mafia members under arrest in Italy

On Friday, March 12th, 1909, Petrosino was shot and killed in Piazza Marina, Palermo. The Piazza was once the execution site of the Inquisition The request to murder Petrosino is said to have come from Lupo the Wolf. Enrico Alfano, the hood beaten up by Petrosino, also claimed credit for "arranging" the killing.

There are several stories relating to the murder. The most credible is that Cascio Ferro, called simply Don Vito in Italy, left a dinner party at the home of a government official and, using his host's carriage and driver, picked up two of his men and drove to Piazza Marina in the Tribunaria/Castellemare district.

They found Petrosino sitting on a small fence that surrounded the garden fountain of Giardini Garibaldi (an equestrian statue of Giuseppe Garibaldi, the Liberator, stands in the garden)

Petrosino was thought to be waiting for an informant that he contacted him earlier in the day and told him to wait in the park. At that point Ferro and men simply walked up to the cop and shot him point blank in the face, killing him and then returned to his dinner party. It was a daylight killing, meaning the Mafia wanted the world to know what had happened. Petrosino was shot four times. One bullet struck him in the throat exiting the nape of the neck, one which struck him in the right shoulder, and one, a massive wound to the right cheek The last wound has been historically attributed to Vito Cascio Ferro who allegedly administered the coup de grace to his hated enemy.

LIEUTENANT JOSEPH PETROSINO.
The Italian detective who was murdered by Black Hand agents in Palermo, Sicily, on Friday evening.

Petrosino's funeral

THE FUNERAL OF THE GREAT DETECTIVE JOSEPH PETROSINO, WHO WAS MURDERED IN PALERMO WHILE TRACKING DOWN ITALIAN CRIMINALS FOR THE NEW YORK POLICE DEPARTMENT

ARRIVAL PETROSINO'S REMAINS   679-14

A nephew, Prospero Petrosino reported that the bullets had been dum-dummed and dipped in garlic so that, even if they did not kill his uncle immediately, he would have subsequently died of blood poisoning. The autopsy report said otherwise. He became the first, and only, New York cop to be killed on foreign soil while on duty.

Another interesting account of the murder comes from Detective Mike Fischetti, (above) Petrosino's protégé who would later assume command of the Italian Squad following its initial disbanding and revival.

Fischetti traveled to Naples, Calabria and Sicily in search of a camorrist murderer named Papaccio and actually lived while undercover with a band of camorristi.

Petrosino

While there he completed Petrosino's mission and collected criminal records of Mafia members wanted by the New York Police. He also investigated Petrosino's murder in the hope of arresting the gunman who had killed his close and dear friend. According to Fischetti, a messenger went to Petrosino telling him a stool pigeon had very important information for him. Obviously, the man couldn't be seen in the restaurant and so Petrosino went out unarmed to meet with him, and as Fischetti recounts: "Petrosino suspected nothing. It was natural for an informer not to want to call on him in the hotel. Petrosino came out and stood talking to the decoy man. The assassin was lurking nearby and stepped up behind him."

Fischetti's information, according to him, came from an Italian nobleman who actually saw the murder from a window in his palace, and watched the detective crumple to the sidewalk and the gunman escape. Fischetti also mentions the gunman was a man called the Schiffizano, because he was involved in the selling of blood of slaughtered animals. Fischetti said the Schiffizano had come to

America after Petrosino's murder and at the time Fischetti had retired, was still living there. Fischetti was never able to learn the Schiffizano's name. Within hours, two men were arrested for the murder but were released due to lack of evidence. Both had been seen in the cafe with Petrosino. Paolo Palazzotto was one of them. His name had been on Petrosino's list and he had been deported from New York by Petrosino for 'Black Hand' crimes in Brooklyn. The other man, Ernesto Militano, was a local Mafia hood.

SHADOW of the "BLACK·HAND".

Vito Cascio Ferro was also arrested four days later but his host insisted that Don Vito had never left his home during the evening and could not have murdered Petrosino. Ferro never denied the murder. He was released without questioning. An informant told the local police that Mafia members Carlo Costantino and Antonino Passananti had returned to Palermo and had been tailing the cop around town. A police intelligence report concluded that Carlo Costantino and Antonino Passananti were the likely murders and that Vito Cascioferro had masterminded the hit.

Vito Cascioferro

In January 1911, almost one year after his imprisonment for counterfeiting, Giuseppe Morello was reported to have spoken to the Attorney representing the US authorities. In the hope of shortening his sentence he supplied information about Petrosino killing in which he blamed Carlo Costantino for the murder. When asked to sign a statement to that effect, Morello refused and the information he had provided was washed from the records. Over 200,000 people attended Petrosino's funeral with a procession that lasted five and a half hours.

THE RUINS OF A FRUIT STORE DESTROYED BY BLACK HAND DYNAMITERS.

On 3rd April, 1909, Vito Cascio-Ferro was arrested in connection with the murder of officer Petrosino. Did Cascio-Ferro murder the cop? Possibly.

Cascio-Ferro

While serving out his life sentence he is reported to have said "Petrosino was a courageous enemy; he did not deserve a dirty death at the hands of just any hired sicario (hit man).

The SPREAD of the BLACK HAND

MILLIONAIRE IS DRIVEN TO EXILE BY BLACK HAND

Italian Murder Methods Now Organizing Throughout the United States.

A Perilous Condition that Must Be Sternly Abolished.

FEAR IN THE BRONX OF THE BLACK HAND

Residents of Washingon Avenue Are Scared by Threatening Letters.

ASK FOR PROTECTION.

NINE DIE BY FIRE

SET BY BLACK HAND.

Blackmail Had Been Refused and Tenement House Was Set Ablaze.

EXPLODE BOMB IN HOUSE WHICH POLICE GUARDED

Black Hand Agents Again Try to Wreck Tenement Owned by Francesco Spinelli.

LIVES OF 10,000 IN PERIL BY BLACK HAND, BINGHAM HELPLESS

BLACK-HAND OUTRAGES CAUSE NEW REIGN OF TERROR

THIS LESSON SPELLED "DEATH"--THOUSANDS IN TERROR SINCE NEW YORK BLACK HAND MASSACRE

He added that he killed the cop "disinterestedly" simply as a matter of honor. A number of bodies were found immediately after Petrosino's murder. Police assumed they were informer working with Petrosino based on the fact that the cop had apparently also had uncovered information that could have only come from people very high up and connected to the criminal justice system in Palermo. There also seems to have been in place a terrorist campaign against police investigating the Petrosino killing and seeking revenge against the New York branch of the Mafia. Pioggio Puccio, a personal friend of Petrosino who helped arrange the funeral and benefit for the detective's widow was murdered a few weeks later. The benefit turned out to be a bust because of threats being sent to performers and donors, and his widow and infant daughter were forced to leave Manhattan due to threats against their lives.

On July 17th 1909, Baldassare Ceola, police commissioner of Palermo was fired from his job. It didn't matter. The dirty work was done. However, Ceola's firing was more political than anything else. He had, in fact, solved the killing in less than three weeks. Ceola's investigation was extremely far-reaching and thorough. Ceola, became embroiled, within a short period, in two of the most sensational assassinations in Italy of his time, that of King Umberto 1 of Italy by Gaetano Bresci, an Italian anarchist who traveled from Paterson, New Jersey to murder the monarch in 1901, and the 1909 Petrosino murder.

Gaetano Bresci

On the same day Theodore Bingham was stepped down as police commissioner of New York. Several people were arrested in connection with the Petrosino killing but were all released on probation or bail. Within a year, all of the charges against them were dropped. By the early 1920s, Ferro's power in the Italian and American Mafia was enormous but it all came crashing down when Benito Mussolini, sensing that the Camorra and Mafia represented more power than his, declared war on the secret Brotherhood.

Benito Mussolini

In 1929, Ferro was arrested for murder. He had been arrested some 69 times and always acquitted. To make sure that didn't happen again, the Fascists framed him. He was sentenced to life in prison. "Gentlemen," he said when it was over, "since you have been unable to find any evidence for the numerous crimes I did commit, you are reduced to condemning me for one I have not."

Blackhand members

Ciro Terranova

Vincenzo and Ciro Terranova's widowed mother was married Giuseppe Morello's widowed father. The Terranova's then, in 1901 arranged for Lupo to marry their sister in 1901. With the Wolfs muscle and influence the Terranova-Morello-Lupo combination were a power to contend with in the underworld Terranova then monopolized the artichoke business. The reign of Lupo and Morello came to an end in 1910 when the two gangsters were convicted of counterfeiting and sentenced to 30 years imprisonment.

They were paroled 10 years later, but in the meantime, the gang passed into the hands of Joe Morello's brothers, Nicholas Morello and Vincenzo and Ciro Terranova. Six years after Petrosino murder in 1909, the Terranova gang still ruled Harlem. But with the 1910 jailing of Lupo the Wolf and Giuseppe Morello, the gang fell under the control of brother, Nicholas Morello.

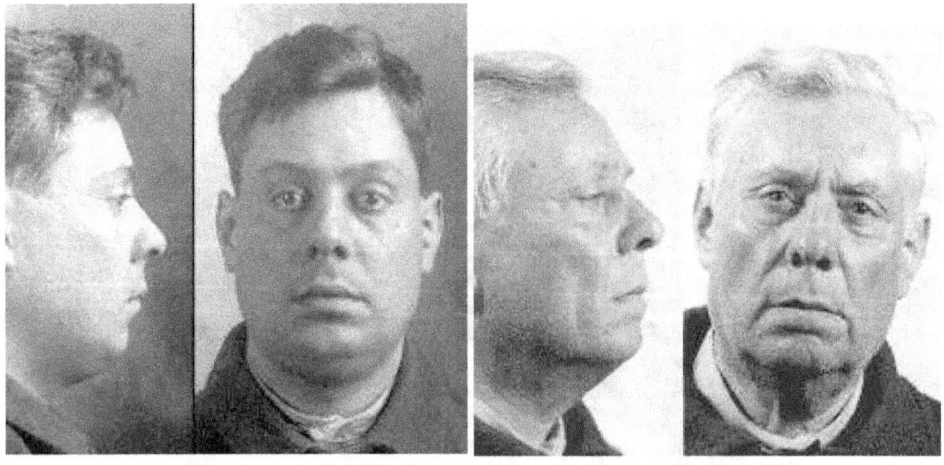

Lupo 1929 and in 1941

The Morello's Harlem Empire was flanked by the Neapolitan Navy St gang headed by Leopoldo Lauritano and Allesandro Vollero, and the Neapolitan Coney Island gang headed by Pelligrino Morano from his Santa Lucia restaurant.

The Navy Street Gang

The gangs worked well with one another and peace ruled to such an extent that every year Andrea Ricci, who headed the Camorra, would hold a 'smoker' each year in Brooklyn with the Morello brothers as his guests.

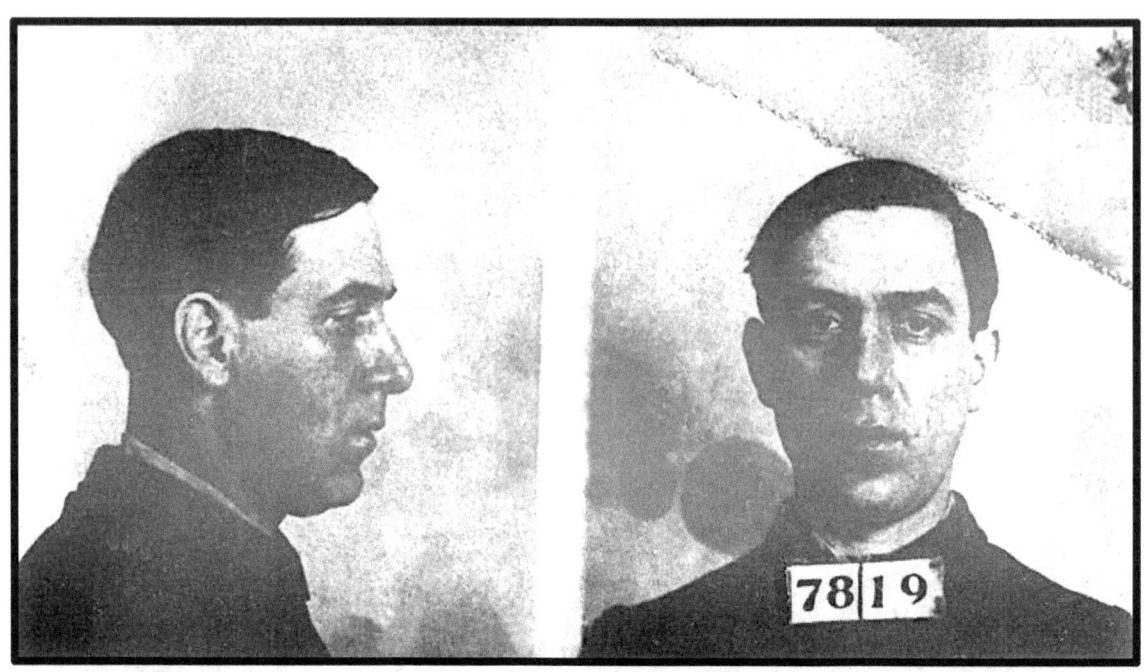

Allesandro Vollero

Once in a while there were problems. When the Neapolitan Del Gaudio brothers, who had connections with the Brooklyn based Navy St gang, traveled into East Harlem to set up gambling operations there, things had to get straightened out. In October of 1914 Nicolo Del Gaudio, was killed after he was lured down to the East River and killed with a shotgun. Joe DeMarco, another gambler left Harlem after a failed attempt on the life of Nick Morello. After two separate attempts were made on his own life, DeMarco moved downtown.

At about that same time, 1916, Giuseppe Masseria was released from prison for a 1913 burglary of a Bowery pawnshop. On June 24th 1916, there was a meeting at Coney Island between the Sicilian Morello gang, the Neapolitan Navy Street gang and the Neapolitan Coney Island gang. The subject at hand was the consolidation of the gangs to control crime in New York, with an eye on gambling, drugs and extortion.

Nick Morello agreed in principle but said that Joe DeMarco would have to be killed before they could control all the gambling lower Manhattan. Three weeks later, the Morello's met with Leopoldo Lauritano from the Navy Street gang at his Cafe to discuss the DeMarco murder. With Nick Morello were his men Steve LaSalle, Ciro Terranova and Giuseppe Verizzano. It was agreed that the Morellos were too well known by Demarco to follow through with the murder so it was agreed that they would use a Navy Street gunmen for the job. They chose John 'The Painter' Fetto for the job, but on the day the killing planned, he showed up to late and the murder was called off.

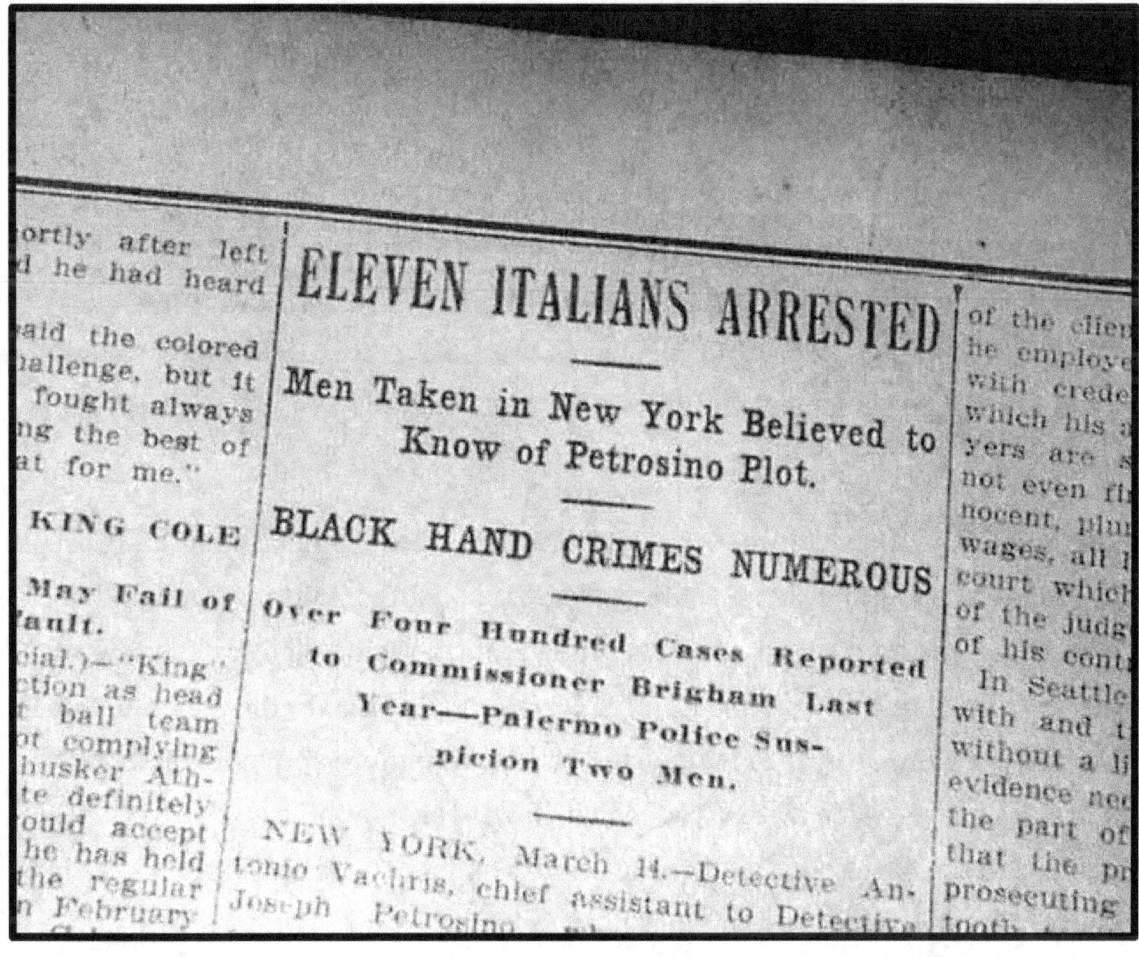

ELEVEN ITALIANS ARRESTED

Men Taken in New York Believed to Know of Petrosino Plot.

BLACK HAND CRIMES NUMEROUS

Over Four Hundred Cases Reported to Commissioner Brigham Last Year—Palermo Police Suspicion Two Men.

NEW YORK, March 14.—Detective Antonio Vachris, chief assistant to Detective Joseph Petrosino

On the morning of July 20th 1916, Louis the Wop, Nick Sassi, Steve LaSalle and Ciro Terranova went to the Navy St café and recruited another of Leopoldo Lauritano's men, Lefty Esposito, to help them kill DeMarco. That afternoon, the Navy Street gunmen, Pagano, Esposito and Fetto set out to one of DeMarco's gambling houses. Although DeMarco had been pointed out to them, the hoods goofed up and in a case of mistaken identity shot and killed a gambler named Charles Lombardi by mistake before they managed to kill DeMarco. Now the Camorra could move into lower Manhattan but there was the business of doing away with the Morello's. Members of the Navy street gang traveled to Philadelphia and meet Andrea Ricci who headed the Camorra and plotted the murder of the Morello gang and control Manhattan on their own. A plan was drawn up to lure the entire Morello leadership down to Brooklyn and ambush them.

On September 7th 1916, Nicholas Morello and Charles Ubriaco traveled downtown to meet with the Navy St gang. In an ambush, both men were killed and the Camorra-Mafia war was on. On October 6th, 1916, Giuseppe Verizzano, another Morello gang member was cut down at the Italian Gardens restaurant in the Occidental Hotel on Broome street.

On Friday the 13th, October 1916, Salvatore DeMarco, brother to the slain Joseph DeMarco, was found dead in a clump of weeds in a lot in Astoria. His skull had been smashed and his throat was cut. The Camorra retaliated by killing four of the Morello gang, with killers imported from Philadelphia. In the meantime, the Navy Street gang prospered and pushed its way into more and more of the Morello's business Joe Nazzaro, who may have been a Morello spy, was kidnapped on March 16th 1917, taken out to Yonkers and killed with his body being left on the nearby trolley tracks.

In May of 1917, Ralph Daniello, a member of the Brooklyn Navy Street gang, was charged with robbery and abduction. He was released for a pending court day but took off to Reno Nevada. He sent letters to the Navy Street Camorra asking for money and legal help but his letters were never answered.   When the police tracked Daniello down in Reno and brought him back to Brooklyn, this time charging him with murder, grand larceny and perjury he began to tell the police everything he knew about the Navy Street crew and the war on the streets. The District Attorney indicted virtually the entire leadership of the Navy Street and Morello gangs as material witnesses.

Site of Giuseppe Morello's murder on Aug. 15, 1930.

By 1920, the Morello-Terranova gang was being challenged by Guiseppe Masseria. Vincent Morello was murdered on East 116th Street and later powerful ally, Umberto Valenti, was ambushed by Masseria gunmen. The Morello gang gave in and joined up with Masseria. Terranova half-brother, Peter "the Clutching Hand" Morello, would become one of Masseria's most trusted lieutenants and Terranova ran upper Manhattan and the Bronx for Masseria during the 1920s.

On April 15, 1931 Terranova agreed to drive a hit squad to the Nuova Villa Tammaro Restaurant in Coney Island. The gunmen, which included Joe Adonis, Albert Anastasia, Vito Genovese, and Bugsy Siegel were working for Lucky Luciano, their victim was Joe Masseria.

Joe the boss

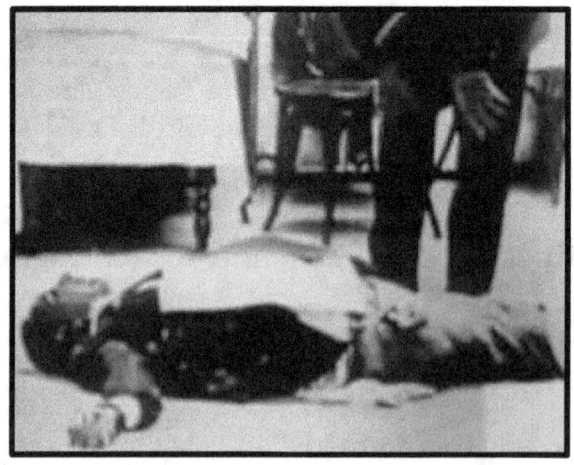

After the killers whacked "Joe the Boss" they rushed back out to the car and found that Terranova was "so shaken that he was unable to put the car in gear." Siegel reportedly shoved him out of the way and took the wheel himself.

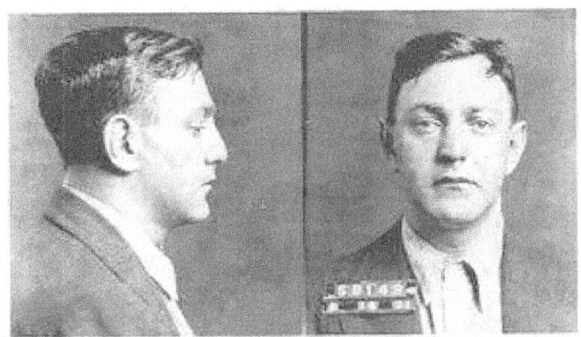

Afterwards, Terranova became partners with Dutch Schultz (Above) in the Harlem number's for 25. That lasted until 1935, when the mob murdered the Dutchman and took his rackets. Terranova's role was replaced with "Trigger Mike" Coppola.

Trigger Mike

Terranova died on February 20, 1938 from the results of a stroke. He was 49 year old and near broke at the time. Peter Morello was killed in his office in August 1930.

Lucky Luciano later claimed that Albert Anastasia and Frank Scalise committed the murders. (All above)

Joe Petrosino